Raising Magic (HUMAN) Mushrooms

A single handbook to wholesome parenting

Snigdha Mallik   Miriam Jacob

Illustrations by Aswathy

First Published in June 2023

ISBN: 978-93-5741-480-7

E-ISBN: 978-93-5819-561-3

BLUEROSE PUBLISHERS

www.BlueRoseONE.com

info@bluerosepublishers.com

+91 8882 898 898

Cover Design:

Tahira

Typographic Design:

Tanya Raj Upadhyay

Distributed by: BlueRose, Amazon, Flipkart

This book is dedicated to our children, who failed to read any of the handbooks before they were born.

A special note from the two (tired yet hopeful!!) authors

It hasn't been easy working on this book with a tight deadline, alongside being mothers and homemakers and doing the million other things that we need to do to keep ourselves and our children thriving (ok, ok, staying afloat to be honest)!

We would snatch even ten or fifteen minutes whenever we could grab those, sometimes while we had our children interrupting every five seconds in the background. One time, one of the children wanted to kill a mosquito with a stone and the editing had to be paused because of the stone hitting the glass (but not the mosquito!).

Even when World War 3 broke out in one of the households between cousins (over an imaginary purse that both were snatching from one another *in imagination*) and continued for two days straight, the editing went on (well, it took a necessary break, but didn't fully stop).

Our illustrator friend has been a huge part of the whole book and we can't thank her enough for bringing the mushrooms to life *and* all the chai sessions - to be honest, book-discussion was a wonderful excuse to meet and eat as well! We sincerely hope that all the chai joints we frequented will always remember the profit we brought to them in the process! May the security at Orion Mall forever keep us in their hearts.

This book coming to completion is a pure miracle in our eyes, and the information here reaching parents and helping children would mean that we have achieved our goal.

We thank you for your patience and love through it all.

Prologue - Mushroom Parenting 101

Too many parenting books

Hello from us! We are Snigdha and Miriam, two mothers trying to give new parents a hand in their roles. Having been through some of this learning process already (spoiler: it never ends), we want to share with you practical tips, tricks, and strategies we have picked up along the way through personal experience. We hope to spare you from having to search through **all** the books and websites that we had to read, and give you a single place to reach out to for the basic information.

When a couple is set out to become parents, they are filled with equal parts excitement and nervousness. Unable to fathom what is to come when the little bundle of joy arrives, the parents-to-be only know that *whatever happens*, they will be ready to shower all the love in the world. However, every step of the way will raise questions and doubts, fears and concerns. How much should my baby sleep, when should I feed solids, hot water for bath or not, is the fussiness normal, how do I respect the child while laying down basic rules, and many many more.

This couple will find themselves overwhelmed with advice upon advice, assertions on what needs to be done to the baby. They will find that there is simply so much material on the internet with countless blogs and accounts that they don't know what to trust and which way to turn. They might be told that there are several books dealing with every single topic - they just have to make time to read them all! Add to this all the mixed advice given by different paediatricians, while WHO seems to be saying something else. And the couple is left flummoxed. They're now scared and stop trusting their own parental instincts (yes, we all have these instincts quite strongly!)

In light of all this available information and also the need to raise the next set of inspired humans with empathy, gentleness and firmness, we bring to you our consolidated perspective towards parenting, putting in *one* book the basic concepts that are there to explore or question about raising children. (For deeper understanding and study of the topics discussed, you can take a look at the references mentioned at the end of chapters, wherever applicable.)

Parenting is no rocket science. However, it is life changing and with the right tools and information, guidance and support, the journey can be a lot more comfortable and worthwhile. In this book, we authors bring to you *Mushroom Parenting*. We would like you to imagine yourself as a mushroom that can gently and firmly hold a child under your shelter and bring them up with love, turning the seeds of future generations into wholesome beings (as you can see on the front cover). We believe the world would be a much happier and empathetic place if we could all be more like those mushrooms.

P. S. We had to stretch our brains to create mushroom-themed chapter titles. If you approve, do let us know on our Instagram accounts (Snigdha @ariensnig_holistic_mommying; Miriam @mj088080)

One book is enough

Table of Contents

Communicating with Your Fungi 1

Handle with Care 9

Unconditional Parenting 26

A Ready-to-Eat mushroom 41

When Little Mushrooms Explode 52

Adult Mushroom Maintenance 81

All the Rest 94

Conclusion to Mushroom Parenting 101 104

Communicating with Your Fungi

Speaking authentically to your child

Language begins in the womb!

You read it right! As their hearing gets better while inside the womb, the child is able to hear what their parents are speaking. They even listen to their mother's voice, the frequent other voices around her (even if hearing is quite dim inside the womb) and the languages that they are speaking.

The child's brain is a powerful tool which enables this fist-sized fella to turn into a non-stop talking machine in a couple of years! It just needs to keep hearing the words, the sentences and the conversations.

The child who is just born may not be able to speak or do anything much but is hearing our language at every moment and assimilating the words slowly. As their vision gets better, they begin to see the objects we point at or look at as we speak and the body language that accompanies our statements. As all of these things are repeatedly noticed, recorded and assimilated by the brain, the context of the conversations slowly starts to sink in for the child. They even pick up on the emotions that go through our face and try to connect it to what we speak. And all of this has started happening in the brain even before the first coherent syllables are being formed by the tongue (directed by the brain, of course!)

Avoid baby language as the primary means of communication: Naming objects with the right words

Let's say that a child's first syllables were Mm or Pp. When the child tries to say something and can only make sounds at the start - take for example "mum-mum" for food - we tend to begin using the same to address food, instead of calling food by the word "food" itself.

However, when we repeat the actual words of objects and speak in authentic, rich language, children can and do catch on! When we read about and understand the concept of the "Absorbent Mind" spoken about by Dr. Maria Montessori, we recognise that one cannot literally see the child absorbing the words that are spoken. However, we know that they don't magically appear out of the child's mouth when the tongue begins to cooperate!

Yes, the child has truly been listening. *And learning.*

They're observing the sentences we speak to them, the language we speak to each other, the songs we sing and the expressions we make!

Just like they watch us walking for months before their body has enough strength to start walking alongside us, they also listen to us for long enough before knowing the words that they need to communicate. During this time, it might not look like any work is happening, but in fact they are absorbing and making sense of it all on the inside.

This also means that if I told my child that I'm her "mother", my child will learn to address me as her "mother". If I simply used the word "father", she would address me in the same way.

Where does this put us?

We may have all heard of the phrase, "*With more power comes more responsibility*". As the adults in the picture here, it becomes our responsibility to talk in the language we want our children to learn. If we only coo back at them, only repeat the same things they tell us, use baby words instead of real words or even if we use expletives casually, these also become part of the absorbing child and his/ her language.

Now think again - with the *power* of being able to talk comes the *responsibility* of talking properly and accurately.

So, the next time that your infant is looking at a dog, ask her if she's looking at a "dog" instead of a "bow-bow". Of course, you can also inform her that the dog makes the sound "bow-bow" or "woof". This helps her learn that the animal in front of her is a dog which is capable of making the sounds you just mimicked. Doesn't that sound better than the child having to learn *bow-bow* to address the dog, only to have to change to the word *dog* itself in some months again?

Multilingualism

What happens in households where families know/ speak multiple languages? Where the mother speaks one language with the child (say Malayalam) and the father speaks another language (say Hindi), and the parents speak to one another in a third language like English, the child will pick up (at least the understanding of) all three languages. You will observe that the child will be able to respond to you in whichever of the three he/ she is comfortable with!

The child who is an expert at assimilating different words and sentences is also capable of learning and differentiating between multiple languages, *provided the languages are not mixed up in the same sentences and conversations.* Then it takes longer and is that much harder.

For example, If I spoke Kannada+English or Hindi+English in the same sentences or conversations (what we locally call *Kanglish* or *Hinglish* respectively), the adult would be able to decipher the meaning as the adult is already fluent with both languages. However this little toddler who is in the process of realising that people speak in separate languages, will have a terribly confusing time in keeping *their* languages pure and clear. Most likely, they would tend to mix up words when trying to converse, have trouble bridging words together vocally while their brain would've gone ahead in a flow and in some rare cases, they may take time to begin talking. The brain has a lot more work to do, trying to put different words of the languages in their places and then figure out which words to respond in!

There was once an infant who was exposed to Marathi by her mother and Kannada by her father. The mother ensured to speak in fluent Marathi alone and the father followed suit in fluent Kannada. This child was able to grasp and bifurcate both the languages and switch efficiently when conversing with the grandparents!

All in all, alongside speaking authentically and genuinely to the child, speaking in clear languages can be highly beneficial in supporting this amazing little brain in the mastery of communication.

Going beyond just words

Of course, communication isn't only about the spoken language. The child is observing your bodily expressions and what words cause what reactions in the adult. It may take years for the child to truly master communication the way the adult uses it but they're at it constantly, improving themselves, learning and registering grammar in sentences, correlating everything to how the adult speaks!

It helps to talk about emotions openly too. To give words to your feelings and explain these to the child. This way, the child truly knows what emotion they're going through. This may seem unnecessary at the face of it but when we think about how many people go through life without realising all their feelings in depth and by suppressing their emotions, we realise how important it becomes to talk of emotions on a daily basis.

After all, emotions are here to stay. The sooner we accept that anger, sadness, jealousy, etc. are as valid as calmness, happiness, humility, etc., the better we fare. By identifying our emotions, we're in a much better place because now we're able to identify the cause of our anger or grief or jealousy. And then we can do something about it or just sit with our body and feelings and tell ourselves that what we're feeling is very much valid. The understanding and communication of this to the child learning all about languages (spoken and body) would be beneficial in the long run.

In summary:

- ❖ Language begins in the womb. A baby can hear dimly whatever the parents are speaking even when inside the womb. Speaking authentically to the child helps during this time too
- ❖ While baby language can be very cute, it helps to name objects with the actual words of the spoken language, rather than words that are used only for the baby

- In households with multilingual caregivers, it helps to talk whole sentences in one language, rather than mixing up the words of two different languages in one conversation
- The baby learns language in a wholesome way - by not just understanding words but also expressions, emotions and the body language of the adult which accompanies their sentences

Books for further study:

The Absorbent Mind, Maria Montessori

Handle with Care

Raising our fungi gently and respectfully

When you hear "gentle parenting", what comes to mind? For many people, it brings up images of children running wild and throwing things, while the parents follow them, cleaning up after the child and apologising to others for destroying their property. A common belief is that gently-parented children have no idea about the consequences of their actions, and grow up very entitled. But this is actually a consequence of permissive - not gentle - parenting.

Difference between gentle and permissive parenting

What is gentle parenting, actually? Put very simply, it is treating children the way any human being would want to be treated, while guiding them how to go about life. This is not to say we treat them like mini adults. No, we treat them with respect while holding developmentally-appropriate boundaries and expectations. For example, it is appropriate to expect a toddler to be very curious and want to touch everything, so we ensure that the space they are in does not give them access to breakable/ valuable/ hazardous items. We cannot leave the electrical socket accessible, then proceed to yell at them when they put their little fingers into it.

We do our best to allow our children to express all emotions, including those which make us uncomfortable (and goodness knows, there are lots of those). This can be intensely challenging, since most of us grew up in environments where our big emotions were not acceptable, let alone respected. To allow our child to let out feelings via shouting and crying feels wrong, somehow. All kinds of worries about spoiling the child arise, and often the adults around us contribute to that. However, I invite you to think about your own experiences of going through something big. Imagine that something has gone disastrously wrong in your workplace, and set you back a long way. Months of hard work has gone down the drain, and you cannot even imagine picking up the pieces and starting again. You go home and find yourself wailing loudly to your partner. Would you prefer them to respond by ignoring or punishing you, so that you don't start getting spoiled - or by holding you physically and emotionally, allowing you to express yourself until the feeling has passed through you? Would you want them to focus on discouraging you from letting out your feelings in future, or give you a safe space to do so?

The basic principle to keep in mind is that all *feelings* are valid and welcome - although not all *behaviours* are. Giving children room to express their feelings does not mean allowing destructive (including self-destructive) behaviour like hitting, kicking, biting or throwing things. In these cases, we can physically block the child from completing the action, and move them away from the scene. As adults, it is our job to keep our children safe, and prevent them from causing harm to others as well.

For the same reason, creating and holding boundaries for everyone's (not just the child's) health and safety is part of our responsibilities. Take the example of brushing teeth. Most children go through a phase (or many phases) of not wanting to have their teeth brushed. As gentle parents, we acknowledge and validate their feelings ("I hear you. You don't want your teeth brushed. You want to keep playing."). And we continue with the process anyway, because as adults, we know that if we don't take care of the child's teeth, it could have lifelong consequences for them ("It's my job to help you stay safe and healthy. I have to brush your teeth now to keep them healthy."). When you've decided to take the gentle parenting route, this feels like forcing and sometimes doesn't sit well. But then, part of our job as adults is to do the right thing even when it is difficult.

Gentle parenting involves a lot of internal work from the parents. Some of this - may be much of this - is very new to us. It doesn't necessarily reflect the way we were brought up. It probably won't feel "right" to have a child express their opinions, to include them in decision making, to offer them choices and not expect them to obey without question. But as with so many other things, once we know better, we try to do better as well. Even if all of it is uncomfortable for us.

Permissive parenting is when the caregiver is unable to say "no" gently and firmly, and feels compelled to say yes to everything their child does! Often this arises from the desire to be gentle parents but not actually understanding how important it is to say no when absolutely necessary. Many of us are scared of the big reactions children may have to being refused things that they want (but which we know are unsafe or unsuitable for them, for example sharp knives or fizzy soft drinks). Some of us may even be afraid that saying no will make our children stop loving us. Most adults are not equipped with tools to hold space for the child's reaction, that is, allowing the feelings to emerge, be fully expressed, and subside. As a result, we end up giving in to avoid the discomfort, and say yes even when we should set a boundary. Difficult as it is to implement, children (all humans, in fact) thrive on healthy boundaries, which is why it is important for us as parents to face this discomfort and work through it.

Consent should be ingrained from the very beginning

Do you like to be asked before someone does something that will affect your body or possessions? Or would you at least prefer to be informed when it is something unavoidable? Definitely, if given a choice, we would all wish to be considered and involved in the process, whether it be something minor like borrowing a pen from us, or something major like a gynaecological exam.

It's the same for children. They are human too. They also may not like it if we adults take it for granted that we can touch their bodies and their things without considering their feelings at all. Even more importantly, respecting their body's autonomy is one of the ways in which we teach them about physical and sexual consent.

As a child, nobody asked me if it was okay to put my pants on me, to squeeze the life out of my cheeks with "love" or even to place a kiss on my face. Most of us grew up thinking that we are at the beck and call of the adults who could do whatever they thought appropriate with a child. "How can the child possibly know what they want?" was a common argument for going ahead and touching children or even taking away their things without asking them first.

Most adults in our generation do not know how to say "No" to being hugged or kissed. We were made to think that love is when somebody wants to hold you (with or without your will) and your denying it simply meant you didn't love them back! I had to undergo this as an emotional blackmail sometimes with my first boyfriend. I wish I had understood then that *I* held the power to say no to even holding his hand.

So, how can we begin teaching something as simple as bodily boundaries to the future generations? Remember, consent starts at home!

Pretty much all concepts start at home.

It's hard to imagine asking your child if you can bathe them or clean them. It must seem like the most obvious thing in the world: why is their permission then needed? It would help to remember that even if their body needs cleaning, it's still *their* body! Hence, you would need to take their consent first. For really small children who do need us to do things for them, we can inform them first - *"I am about to give you a bath to clean your body. You can let me know if you feel uncomfortable at any point..."*

If you think you're laying too much power in their hands, consider this - the only power you're giving them is the one over *their own bodies*, which they should have from the start anyways.

There was a lady who pinched my daughter's cheek a few days back. Her intention was expressing love towards my child. My daughter hates being touched on her face and instantly reacted with a loud "Don't touch me!". The lady was taken aback and said, "I only did it out of love" and looked towards me, waiting for me to reprimand my child for reacting that way.

I looked from my child whose cheeks had been squeezed without consent, to the lady who thought adults have the right to touch any child as they wish simply under the canopy of "love" and I told her that my daughter doesn't like being touched on her face and requested her not to do it again. With the angry woman glaring at me, I told my daughter that it's okay to tell someone not to touch her if she doesn't like it and to also block them the next time if she sees it coming. She could offer alternatives like shaking their hand if she was comfortable with that.

Do we go around pinching the cheeks of every lady we think is cute or demanding a hug from every handsome man that *we* find humorous? When it's ridiculous to have such expectations of an adult, why is the same courtesy not extended to children? Their rights should not be taken for granted either.

If consent isn't practised right from the start, the child who will eventually grow into a teenager with raging hormones or an adult with a need for connectivity, will not be able to say no when somebody abuses them in the name of "Love". And equally, they may not value another person's consent.

Remember that most abuse happens under this pretence and by known people. Hence it's very important to bring up a child who understands that love doesn't mean doing only what *you* want with the person you love. Love also means respect and boundaries, asking for permission and understanding personal space!

How mistakes are treated from a gentle parenting perspective

What would you wish for a child to learn *after* making a mistake? What do you wish for them to learn about how to treat *others* who have made a mistake? How do *you* wish to be treated after making a mistake?

It feels odd to treat children the same way we treat adults, but remember that that is the basis of gentle and respectful parenting. We would not want our college professor or boss at the workplace to scream at us and punish us for making a mistake (leave alone hitting us).

We would not think that is the best way for us to learn, would we? It shouldn't be any different for children. The only difference is that they have a lot more to learn, since everything is new for them.

If a bowl of water is spilled on the floor and everybody starts yelling, "Look what you did!" or "So much mess" or "Can't you be careful??", the poor child is scared out of their wits and feels like they did something that brought on the end of the world!

All we need to do is tell the child:

"Oh I see that the bowl dropped and there is water on the floor" (non-accusatory tone)

"We don't want anyone to slip on this water and fall" (consequences of spilt water)

"Let's get the mop and clean it up" (how to correct a mistake).

Mistakes are normal, and part and parcel of life. Nobody is perfect and it is human to err. When we can normalise mistakes, we find that forgiveness comes easier to us and we will look at problem-solving rather than playing the "blame-game".

If you wouldn't do it to an another adult, it probably isn't okay to do to a child

He hit her across the cheek. In the next few minutes, her cheek turned red and tears welled up in her eyes. A friend saw her swollen cheek and asked her to report the abuse to the cops.

Who did you imagine when you read the above lines? A man hitting a woman? What was your reaction? I am certain that you felt indignant at the slapping action. You may even have felt like you needed to avenge the poor helpless woman.

What if I told you that the above was written in the context of a little girl?

Read it again.

Does that make one think that the parent must have been justified somehow in punishing their child? If the general reaction of the society is that the child must have deserved it in some way, we need to evaluate what we classify as "abuse" in our society. If *only* an adult hitting another adult is looked upon as physical abuse, the entirety of the children's population is not even considered as "people" then.

Where the child must be given extra importance in our lives as they hold the future to humanity, they are instead looked down upon as insignificant.

We assume that the adult needn't show respect to the child or their body, that the child's existence isn't valid enough until they are grown up. The adult is too busy paying attention and making rules that suit the existing adult, instead of trying to protect the interests of the *future adult.*

Stand up for your child

It takes a village to raise a child.

Yes, a village can be very very helpful! When we're a part of joint families or part of very closely held communities, it often happens that we have to take a lot of others into consideration. Or so we believe!

Especially when it comes to a newborn, *everybody* has an opinion. *Everybody* thinks they have the right to take offence if their forced suggestions weren't followed through.

When I tell the massage lady that I do not want her pouring extremely hot water on my little child or me, I don't mean it as a "maybe". I mean it as a "No" to hot water.

In some cultures, boundaries are usually very blurred. Especially in nations where the populations are very high and the understanding of space is already low, people tend to push over a "No" and just do what they please.

Imagine this below example from an adult's perspective: My child is crying when being bathed with hot water. I need to step in, tell the person who is bathing the child to make the water less hot right this instant. And as a parent, I would also need to soothe my child. If the person drawing up the bath/ bathing the child is unable to follow or chooses to ignore my instructions, then I would need to probably restrict their access to the bathing water or to the child itself.

That is how setting a boundary and implementing it with adults looks like.

Meanwhile, let's take a look at the entire situation from the child's eye: *The water is very hot, my skin feels like it's burning and I begin to do what I can do best to call for help - I begin crying. My parent steps in, stops the hot water bath, soothes me and dries me up. I can see my caregiver standing up for me and this gives me hope. I now know that help is available when I need it.*

Simply seeing their parents stand up for them can be very empowering for children. Why should children be empowered, you ask? Simply so that they can stand up for themselves as an adult! A lot of adults cannot say "No" and often find themselves in unpleasant situations. Saying no where necessary is a life skill and like everything else, it starts with setting examples at home.

A lot of times, we would need to demonstrate standing up for ourselves or the child with close family members and people in the local community. This is probably the hardest but also very necessary to keep relationships healthy.

There is an old man close to our house. Most children run away when he comes storming down the road. One evening, while I was carrying my child, he came along and I could feel my daughter tense up. Knowing that he didn't understand physical boundaries, I tried stepping away from him while carrying her. He still put out his long arms and pinched her cheeks. My daughter who is usually very vocal about this was scared to even say anything to this intimidating man. On her behalf, I told him not to pinch her cheeks as she didn't like it. However, he took it as a challenge and said, "Why shouldn't I pinch her cheeks? Watch me do it."

(Note that this situation had already become an object of testing his ego at this point - at least in his head - and wasn't even about the child anymore!)

As he put out his hand again, I had to literally push away his hand and keep her face safe. The child breathed a sigh of relief as he cursed under his breath and walked off.

If your child does *not* want to be touched, it is not okay to touch him/ her, unless it is for a medical reason or something unavoidable, of course. We are the parents and protectors, after all. However this right cannot extend to everybody and not even to us once they know how to bathe themselves and to wash their private parts and don't want us to do it.

We do not have to pick a fight with the other adults at all times: that is not what standing up for what we believe in means. It helps to pick and choose our battles and to also really know our non-negotiables and communicate the same authentically, firmly and politely (at least the first time around!!). After all, the people in our village are genuinely trying to help us with whatever knowledge they possess. It can help to share the up-to-date information that we are aware of with them and to equip them with this knowledge as well. A lot of times, modelling what we want to see is useful with adults as it is with children.

For example, when we choose to follow baby-led weaning when introducing solid food, this can be met with a lot of resistance from people of older generations who are only used to feeding children, sometimes forcibly. It is ingrained in them that children are not capable of knowing how much to eat, hence need to be fed. However, as children develop the skills needed to hold food, use cutlery, and feed themselves to their hunger, these same people have been known to come back and praise baby-led weaning! They marvel at the child's capabilities.

When raising a child within a tribe/ community, alongside laying boundaries and holding them constant, it also works to acknowledge the help and love that the members of the community bring to the parent and the child. Let them know that the parent holds the ultimate responsibility of the child while appreciating all their help and support.

Privacy

Privacy and personal space can be a blur in some societies. To understand why an individual needs privacy can become hard. However, it is important to understand that we don't always have to be told *why* privacy is important to an individual and should be able to support them if this is their ask.

For a small child, this can range from going to the bathroom on their own to closing the door when they want to wear clothes. The safety rules we make around this would be as simple as not letting a little child bolt the door when they want to be alone, limiting and listing out the number of people who get to change their clothes or wash their private parts.

As they grow older, they may want to write in a journal which is banned to the adults in the picture or even bathe by themselves. It is important to understand and respect these boundaries for the child. How else can they learn to respect other people's privacy and personal space?

I once heard of an old lady who was incharge of her daughter and grandson. She took this job so seriously that she washed the boy's hair until he was about 15 years old. The catch here is that the boy kept saying "No". The old lady said that she did it out of "Love" anyway.

However, consider this. What did the boy learn through his formative years? That love meant to overstep any physical boundaries. What can be the consequence of this? That he may very well not understand how to give his friends or partners their private space or respect their physical asks in the future! It is very important to evaluate what sort of example we are setting for the little ones watching us.

As they grow into teenagers, they will explore their bodies and want to do so behind closed doors. The best we can do is keep conversations open (ranging from talking about our days or our emotions to listening to our children with genuine interest), set down rules for the house and encourage bonding by doing activities together as a family, like eating meals together. These things can create an atmosphere of mutual trust and respect.

As with everything else we have been discussing, the basic rule is to respect the rights of children just as much as we do for adults - bearing in mind their health and safety, of course.

In summary:

- ❖ It is essential to know the difference between gentle and permissive parenting. Gentle parenting is raising a child with respect, empathy and firm boundaries. Permissive parenting is giving in to the child without holding any consistent rules or boundaries
- ❖ The concept of consent should be practised at home and ingrained in our parenting style right

from the beginning. This helps children understand and respect their own space and that of others as they grow up

- ❖ Mistakes are common to being human. They are treated as such in the gentle parenting approach and the child is able to see how to apologise and make amends (if any are possible/necessary) when mistakes are made
- ❖ If something is not okay to be done to another adult, it most likely is not okay to be done to a child either. It helps to remember that the child is a complete person
- ❖ Standing up for the child goes a long way in helping the child draw boundaries for themselves as they grow up. It empowers the parent and the child in putting into practice the parenting that they want to practise as a family
- ❖ Privacy is an important aspect of being human. Everybody requires personal space and privacy to do certain things (as long as they aren't harmful - and this has to be taught young). In gentle parenting, we respect the rights of another person wanting their privacy, be it an adult or a child

Books for further study:

Kiss Me: How to Raise Your Children with Love, Carlos González

Unconditional Parenting

Loving our little mushrooms for who they are

What is unconditional love?

The kind of love that doesn't need any conditions to be met in order to be given out, the kind of love our pets feel for us, the kind of love we feel for our little ones even after they're not-so-little anymore, is it not?

Then why is our parenting slathered with so many layers of conditions in it?

Shouldn't unconditional love equal unconditional parenting as well?

Unfortunately, it is found that many a times, we do not know what unconditional parenting actually looks like - to not threaten the child or not to bribe him/ her, to not rank everything that the child does and to not make everything a competition.

Do my above sentences trigger you? Maybe we should look at this in slightly more detail, you and I. Parent to parent.

Different forms of motivation: intrinsic versus extrinsic

What's the first thing that comes out of our mouth when our child puts on their trousers by themselves?

"Good job" or "Good boy" or "Good gal"!

What do we mean? That they simply did an amazing job by putting on their trousers on their own.

How does the child perceive it? That they are good somehow simply because *we* approve of what they did (their action of putting on their pants).

How does this translate to other things in life? As we keep dishing out this kind of praise to the child, they're getting more attuned to thinking that their goodness actually comes from the *actions* that they're performing and the approval they are receiving from the adults. Whereas, aren't they innately good anyway?

Aren't their actions determined by their goodness and not the other way around?

So, in reality, what sort of people are we creating? Those who start deciding if they're "good" (or good enough) based on the acknowledgment given by others. Worse yet, they decide their worth based on what others think/ say about them! Can you imagine that? Haven't we all lived like that at some point in our lives?

Consider a simple scenario for better understanding. Let's say that I'm an artist and I've created a piece of art with all my heart and you are the viewer for it. If you think that my piece of art is good, I thank you with all my heart for taking the time to view it. But does it mean that *I'm* good enough? What if you didn't like my art and didn't say "Good job"? Would it have lessened my worth somehow or made my efforts any less potent?

Think of a generation that does amazing things because it makes *them* happy, not because someone else may like it and praise them for it. The world would then be a much happier place. Like, if I danced with all my heart but my Instagram reel of this only received 50 hearts, this shouldn't take away the joy of my dance! It would be truly sad if it did! It would be worse if I thought of myself as unworthy because I didn't get enough likes or comments from others! I should be dancing because it brings *me* joy. And along the way, if I can spread this joy to a few others, then so be it.

We are worthy simply because we exist, not because of the things we "achieved" or because someone else deemed us worthy. And in order to create a child who believes in themselves irrespective of their circumstances, we can take a stand today and give the child those compliments that bring the focus onto the work of the child itself. Like, "you did it all on your own" or "you did it with some help" or "you have been trying so consistently, your efforts have brought you so far".

Think of the motivation these lines can bring to a child, in place of motivation that comes from seeking external approval. This can be a game changer for both the child and the parent, the ultimate goal being that the child should be intrinsically motivated, have faith in themselves, and find joy within, rather than just keep looking for external appreciation all their life.

Rewards to get things done can set the expectation of doing things only if given something

More often than not, we make statements like "If you clean your room, you can have ice cream". Whereas, we didn't need to relate the dessert to cleaning of the room because the room needs to be clean to maintain general hygiene!

We offer rewards in an attempt to control certain outcomes, like having the wilful toddler keep their floor mat clean always (which is completely un-childlike) or get the rebellious teenager to put all their clothes into the wardrobe! However it is not desirable or realistic to attempt to have everything in our control this way.

Some of the few things that are actually in our control are:

- ❖ Setting an example by keeping *our* spaces clean and organised and doing this cleaning in front of the child

- Keeping a limited number of toys available to the child at any given time
- Offering to help the toddler in the chore of cleaning up, folding up, winding up, etc. after any activity is done or at the end of the day and making it a team effort, so that they don't feel that the boring task only falls upon them
- Making cleaning a fun activity, like having a song for it or making a game out of putting all the books back or saying goodnight to each of the toys as we lay them back into their basket

When we offer rewards for these daily activities, the understanding of why the activity should be done in the first place is taken away. The reason behind having a bath or cleaning up the room shouldn't be lost. The use of rewards only results in manipulating children into doing the activity without understanding the real need for it to be done. Also, if resistance builds to the offered rewards, the rewards would need to get bigger and better, or other methods would need to be concocted, making the whole process that much harder!

Let's try a hypothetical experiment: imagine that I suddenly call upon my friend's daughter, who is very fond of drawing. She likes to draw and colour all day. I tell her, "If you draw well, I will give you a prize". I continue to do this for 5 days. Every day she draws something remembering that she will be given a prize for it at the end of the day.

Is her mind on the drawing or on the reward itself?

After 5 days, I tell her, "All prizes are over. Even if you draw something beautiful today, I will not be able to give you an award."

What happens at this point? This child has become accustomed to drawing in order to be rewarded. The lack of an award suddenly makes her feel empty and uninspired from within. She no longer wants to randomly draw and colour like she used to, unless there is a competition or the expectation of a reward.

What has actually happened here? We have taken a child who loves drawing and colouring and made her want to draw only if a carrot is dangled in front of her in the name of a prize. We have successfully converted intrinsic motivation into extrinsic motivation! The happiness that depended on herself now depends on somebody else.

The repercussions of offering rewards for every small activity can kill the joy that comes from inside for doing the same activities. It can also squash the motivation to do some of the basic daily things in life like cleaning up, doing laundry, brushing teeth, keeping footwear outside, etc.

Instead of just saying "Nice" or "Good", we can genuinely observe and ask relevant questions

A lot of times, our child has sat for hours drawing what look like random lines and filling random colours on their sheets/ books. And when they show these to us and look at us for our remarks as if their worlds hang on it, the least we can do is take a genuine look at what they've done and give them thoughtful feedback like, "I see you've put in so much effort to create this." or "You've used a lot of colours here. Do you like when things are more colourful?". Use real observations. Phrases such as "Good job" or "Nice work" make them feel good temporarily but they don't know if we meant what we said. However, they will find more specific and detailed observations made by us far more meaningful.

To continue with the example of a child's artwork, it is essential to remember that art needn't be a certain way! After all, everybody's imagination is different. We are used to seeing things done in a stereotypical way, for example, leaves are always green and the sky is always blue. This makes it very tempting for us to be a critic and point out what we see as flaws or mistakes when a child shows us their work. However, consider this - if a child can think out of the box and follow their imagination, isn't this something we want to encourage (and not just in art)?

We can even ask them questions about the work they did, why they drew a certain thing or if any of the lines in their work had any significance. These help us understand their work better and make them think about why they did something a certain way and if they could've done it differently.

If a child helped somebody out of genuine empathy, saying "good job" can misplace the source of their empathy on external factors. It can go on to make the child want to help someone simply to be told these very words! If we can instead point out the emotions of happiness or capability felt by the child in helping a person out and the emotions of gratitude felt by this very person in receiving the help, the child would be more connected to why they would want to help somebody in the future.

Punishments are not as necessary as adults have come to believe

I will always remember something that my therapist pointed out to me: time-outs came at an age when there was a lot of violence against children and a more non-violent system of *punishments* had to be evolved, for the sake of the little child!

Human society has gone through immense changes over time. Amidst all the aspects that evolution touched, our point of interest - which is parenting - has been undergoing a constant change. Take for example, *respect*. This often was not extended to children, but is now being made an integral part of parenting. Because, people now realise that *what children see, they will do!*

Lead by example. If they see violence, they will learn that violence against the powerless is okay. If they see "detachment-punishment" (a term I prefer using to describe "time-out" better), then they will see that it's okay to detach emotionally when something goes wrong. Whereas, we want our children to learn to connect to their emotions. And process those emotions! Not detach completely when something goes amiss...

Let's take one common example. When your child is hitting you/ another child/ someone else, what happens if you put your child in a timeout by sending them to their room or an isolated corner? They get isolated physically *as well as emotionally*. You want them to regulate themselves but they don't know how. You want them to think about the hitting they did and why it's not okay to harm somebody, but unless the adult is able to calm them down and tell them, how can the child know by themselves what was wrong with just expressing themselves? In fact, expression is not wrong but it simply depends upon the form of expression. Sitting in their room by themselves, the child cannot come upon this simple truth.

Punishments like time-out without the parent being present to regulate can be emotionally disturbing.

What is it that you would need to do then? When the hitting commences, block your child physically. Contain the child within your arms gently but firmly if need be. And in order to regulate a child who is feeling his/ her emotions so intensely (yes, every emotion is very intense for this little hooman), the adult would themselves need to be regulated first.

For most of us, many things children do are triggering simply because our inner child remembers the times we were severely reprimanded or punished by being hit or being threatened when little! We weren't allowed to express ourselves freely and whether we like it or not, during times of intense emotions, we tend to reflect what we saw and experienced *as children,* on our children as well.

So take a deep deep breath, let your inner child know that this isn't happening to you right now. Generally, calming your inner child, or speaking to them at neutral times can help identify the triggers and be regulated enough to be in an intense situation with your unregulated child as described above.

A regulated adult can hold boundaries better by using statements such as "I can see you're very upset right now. Hands are not for hitting" or "I will need to help contain you until you are in a position to not harm anyone". What you're doing here is letting the child know that you see and feel them and their emotions, and also tell them that the boundary of not-hitting is in place. You can remove the child to another place if that's better and instead of leaving the child alone seething or angry or upset in a "time out", sit along with the child, be there for them, offer comfort, acknowledge their feelings and help them regulate.

Co-regulation is the key to parenting. After all, a little child's frontal lobe isn't developed enough to process these extreme emotions and be regulated at the same time. They are physically and mentally unable to contain their impulses and hence would need a calm adult to help do this with them! It helps to remind ourselves that the child and the parent are on the *same team*, as opposed to punishments which make the child feel like the parent is working *against them.*

Not pushing children to excel out of our own fears and feelings of not-enoughness

A lot of times, we are pushing our children towards perfection simply because *we* believe that perfection is the ultimate goal. We forget to realise as well as convey to our children that the experiences along the way matter too. We think that helping them achieve what *we* couldn't is the best thing that we can do for them and in the process, we forget to consider what our children themselves want.

We end up projecting our dreams on to the child and hoping for them to achieve those things we never could. When we do not feel good enough (or we feel like underachievers), the feeling of satisfaction or achievement is pursued under the garb of our children. If they achieve something we couldn't, we then feel satisfied. *But at what cost?* If the child's pursuits and skillset, likes and dislikes are ignored, then even this sense of achievement that we end up feeling comes at a very very high price - the cost of the child's purpose itself!

If a child wants to be a drummer but we push them towards another field that is either close to our heart or a field that we consider more lucrative, where do you think the *child's* heart will truly lie as they grow up? As they come to understand themselves or believe that it's too late to pursue their life's goal, the blame would rightfully fall upon the adult who was unable to respect the child's ability to choose.

Even if it wasn't a matter of choosing fields or interests, pushing children to simply rank higher in their own class or score more marks than their peers can become such a burden to this carefree and energetic being that exists inside every little child. Pushing them to *excel* instead of helping them to *learn*, can take away all the joy and curiosity out of the material in front of them. It can also end up changing their focus to competition rather than learning.

Abuse/ neglect are noticed and copied by children

There was a party at a friend's place one day. A lot of pretend play was in progress amongst the slightly older set of kids. The oldest girl then took the leather belt from her father and pretended to hit all the other kids saying, "You've been bad. You deserve to be punished."

The children laughed, the adults in the room laughed. No one batted an eyelid.

However, isn't this a display of what is happening to the children behind closed doors? If a woman or man (or any adult) were beaten up under the label of "punishment", we would instantly term it as *abuse* and the perpetrator wouldn't get away with it. When it's a child, why is the label of *punishment* deemed okay?

What is the message that all the children received at the party that day? That "punishment" is okay if the authority figure believes that somebody did wrong. In a nutshell, it becomes all about the power resting with the person in-charge and how they use (or misuse) it!

What about the silent audience that didn't say anything and laughed it off as child's play? Not speaking up when something isn't right is equivalent to saying loud and clear that we accept what is happening in front of us. It is important to be conscious of the unspoken messages that we convey to our children, because what we normalise becomes their normal.

In summary:

- ❖ Unconditional parenting is a form of parenting that comes with unconditional love, so that the child can move towards being naturally caring and understanding of their role at home and in society
- ❖ The different forms of motivation are intrinsic and extrinsic motivation. Unconditional parenting often promotes the growth of intrinsic motivation which is desirable for a person's happiness in the long run
- ❖ When we offer rewards to the child to do something that they liked doing anyway, we are

taking away the joy of doing this from their heart. When it's a daily life task that is rewarded, we take away an understanding of the necessity to do these tasks

- ❖ How then do we go about showing our appreciation? By making real life observations on the child's work and bringing to their attention the emotions felt by all parties involved when any help was extended by the child
- ❖ Punishments which are often deemed necessary by adults can make the child feel like the parent is working against them. It would help to tackle any problem *together*, rather than by punishing a child for it
- ❖ Often adults push children to excel, out of their own feelings of not being enough. It is best to let the child do *their* best, not what the adult labels as "best"
- ❖ Abuse or neglect under the label of punishment can be easily copied by children. It is best to avoid physical punishments like spanking and emotional punishments like timeouts altogether

Books for further study:

Unconditional parenting, Alfie Kohn

A Ready-to-Eat Mushroom

Starting solids

Weaning is the process of introducing regular solid foods into a baby's diet, (very) slowly replacing breast/ formula milk until the child is no longer consuming it at all. Sounds simple, doesn't it? And it can be - but often ends up causing immense stress and anxiety for many parents, mainly because of our beliefs and expectations around the subject. Also the pressure we feel around it (self-imposed or coming from outside) doesn't help!

Over the generations, the famines that hit humans, seasons of floods and other natural calamities have made us genetically and historically more aware of the periods of *lack of food.* With this knowledge ingrained within us subconsciously, we tend to think that food must always be made a priority, food must be stuffed into people, good hosts are those who offer lots and lots of food, and babies absolutely need to be full all the time in order to take humanity physically forward! Sometimes without realising it, we equate eating a lot with being healthy.

A human being is so much more than just what they eat. A human baby especially is learning several new things of which he has no prior knowledge, absorbing even the minutest details from his environment. He is quick to repeat and is filled with raging emotions that he's yet to understand. They're getting new teeth and growing in sudden spurts. Yes, eating forms an essential part of all of this... but remember,

Eating isn't Everything!
A baby is NOT a walking stomach!

'Eat, eat, eat' he said.
'I've eaten!' I pleaded.
'You disrespect me?!' He threatened.
'I'm full' I begged.
'Please won't you eat another bite?' he coaxed.

'My stomach hurts' I cried.
'One bite for you, one for mamma, one for grandma...' he played.
'I simply cannot' I vomited.
'Aeroplane' he whirred:
'I'm tired,' I whispered.
'You don't love us' he manipulated.
I wept and raged at the adult who wouldn't listen,
As he placed yet another plate of food in front of me.
'Eat, eat, eat' he said.
'I've eaten!' I pleaded...

Let's not turn eating food into an experience our children would rather forget. Let's not jeopardise their relationship with food, and their long-term health. Introducing solids without pressure and without negative associations is essential, as is allowing them to mindfully experience the food and the process of eating. Distraction methods end up getting more food into the child, but at what cost? Life is not an eating competition, after all. And in adulthood, so many of us have had to re-train ourselves to eat consciously, eat only as much as we need, not distract ourselves with screens while eating, and so many other habits we recognise as not beneficial to our health. Why not start our children off the right way, instead of creating unhelpful associations which they will need to break later in life?

There was a child we knew, who was given sweetened food whenever normal food was rejected and lots of chocolates in the second year just to get through the rejection phases. This child lost interest in eating family food and his association towards food ended up being that he wanted sweet all the time. It took the family years to realise what they had done and then try breaking this unnatural association with food.

When we both had been to a restaurant recently, we saw a child who wouldn't look at her plate until a phone was dangled in front of her. Once the food started going inside, she had no idea *what* she ate or even *how* much she ate. We are probably all familiar with this experience, when we have eaten a meal in front of the TV, for example. This is clearly not the best way to cultivate mindful eating.

Let us talk about starting solids. There are two ways we can go about it:

The traditional weaning method

The baby led weaning method

What is Traditional Weaning?

In the traditional weaning method of starting solids, we feed the baby, and usually begin with mashed food rather than whole pieces. We might offer food in a spoon, or with our hands. It is important to note that this is done responsively, meaning we wait for the child to show interest, to move towards the spoon or our hand, and take the food from it. Shoveling food into a distracted child's mouth is a big no-no! So the typical strategies of "look, there's a crow/ aeroplane/ butterfly" and pushing the spoon to the child's mouth while they are looking into the sky are not the way to go.

If you start with traditional weaning, the aim is to move the child onto regular food of a regular texture by the time they are a year old. So even if you begin weaning with mashed food, you fairly soon need to make it more textured. This is quite important in order to avoid the chance of the child rejecting regular food later on because they are not comfortable with the feel of it (and have ended up becoming used to only mashed/ puréed food).

What is Baby Led Weaning?

Baby-led weaning is quite straightforward. Rather than beginning with purées and then changing textures each month or so, we begin by offering food from the family pot right away - starting with vegetables, then fruits. Introduce proteins and grains whenever you are comfortable - note that some children take longer to adjust to digesting these and may become constipated. So observe and follow your child.

The size and shape of pieces of food might need to change for the baby, to make it easier for them to grasp (based on palmar or pincer grasps) and to avoid choking hazards. Some things would need to be cooked for longer before being served (to be soft enough for the child to manage), but otherwise the child is offered basically what the family is eating without salt/ sugar for the first year.

One reason people can be reluctant to follow baby-led weaning is the belief that babies have no teeth and therefore cannot chew solid food. However, an infant without teeth is not the same as an elderly person who has lost their teeth. Infants have a whole set of milk/ deciduous teeth under their gums, which are waiting to erupt in time. They can most definitely chew food. Anyone who has ever had a teething baby chomp on their finger can testify to this.

There is a wealth of information on this subject available online. Often the hardest part of implementing baby-led weaning is being subjected to the opinions of those who think you're starving the child! In fact, this method is the easiest way to ensure that the child eats exactly as much as they need at any given time, because they are fully in control of the quantity that goes in.

We have both followed baby led weaning with our daughters and are thankful for the healthy eating habits that this method has helped our children to develop! Whenever either of us go to a restaurant or a function, we are thankful that we can sit together with the child as a family and eat (whenever the child is hungry), instead of having to run behind the child to feed them.

General Guidelines for weaning

- Before starting solids, consider the signs of readiness - completion of 180 days of age, loss of tongue thrust, being able to sit up in the tripod position for a few seconds at least
- Using a high chair or booster chair for meal times can be very helpful. It helps the child to understand that eating happens in one place
- Eating together as a family, or at least one carer with the child, helps teach the child about ways of handling food when eating it (chewing, using

cutlery, etc), and can be an enjoyable bonding experience too

- Offer new food items in the first half of the day, so that if your child reacts to them, you will not be rushing to the hospital in the middle of the night
- Regarding introduction of common allergens, or any food which your family has a history of allergy to, please discuss with your paediatrician
- Avoid animal milk as a drink until at least age of one
- Avoid soups, juices and other very watery foods in the first year at least, as they will end up replacing the more nutritional breast milk/ formula milk
- No added salt or sugar: the kidneys of infants are not sufficiently developed to process added salt, and added sugar is anyway not a necessary part of anyone's diet. Besides, infants already have a preference for sweet tastes, and we ideally need to expose them to other flavours in the first year, when they are more likely to try new things. For this reason, we suggest offering vegetables first before starting on fruit, and avoiding sweetening other food by adding fruit to it
- Expose the baby to a wide range of food (lots of colours and textures) before the age of one to increase acceptance: after one year of age, children are much less likely to try new items and flavours. Hence, try to offer as much variety as possible in the

first year, so that many things are already familiar to them by the time the rejection phase strikes

- Family pot by one year: regardless of which weaning method you choose, the child should be offered family food by one year. Continuing mashed or puréed foods for too long increases the chances of them rejecting regular food
- Normalise rejection of food: children will not overnight start eating solid food instead of breast/ formula milk. Weaning is a process, and it is a much longer one than most of us expect. Children will reject food, spit it out, throw it on the floor, mash it into their hair, and do everything but eat. Occasionally a bite might actually be chewed and swallowed. This is normal. **Until at least one year, breast/ formula milk remains their primary source of nutrition. The quantity of liquid feeds should not reduce**
- Following on from the above point, offer milk feeds before solids (until one year of age). Breast milk should be offered 30-45 minutes before solids, and formula 60-90 minutes before solids. This is to ensure that the quantity of milk feeds is maintained, and that the child is sufficiently hungry for the solid food
- No distraction or force feeding: we know eating mindfully and listening to our bodies regarding the quantity required is the best thing for adults. It is

the same for children. They are very much capable of understanding their body's requirements and hunger. We just need to offer them nutritionally dense food

When we feel like our child isn't eating enough, is rejecting way too much, is unable to finish the food on their plate, remember that the adult's perception of quantity (which cannot be applied directly to a child) may need to change here. Babies are far more in sync with their own bodies and most often, even one or two bites is enough to get them happily through the day! Regardless of what we adults might feel, children who have sufficient access to food and are developing normally will not starve themselves.

So, remember to remind yourself that it is your job to *offer* wholesome food, and it is the child's role to decide *which* of that food they want and *how* much they want to eat.

In summary:

- ❖ Weaning is the process of (slowly) moving children off an exclusive milk diet (breast milk or formula) onto solid food.
- ❖ Babies are not just stomachs to be filled. It can be tempting to try and stuff them with food, but this doesn't help to create healthy and positive associations with food.

- Traditional weaning usually involves an adult responsively feeding the child with mashed or puréed food.
- Baby-led weaning usually involves providing the child with food in shapes and textures which are appropriate for them to hold and bite/ chew on their own.
- There are several important general guidelines which apply regardless of which weaning method you follow, including waiting for them to show all the signs of readiness to start, not adding salt or sugar until they are at least a year old, avoiding animal milk as a drink until one year of age, and bringing the child onto regular family food by completion of one year.

Books for further study:

My Child Won't Eat, Carlos Gonzalez (more specifically related to weaning)

Sapiens, Yuval Noah Harari (a general overview of how millennia of history affect us even today)

When Little Mushrooms Explode

Toddler rebellions and meltdowns

You must have surely heard of the phrases "terrible twos" or even "frightening fours". But I ask you - *terrible for whom?* This child who is just two years old has to navigate our world ridden with adult rules and ways of life. When the child tries to express themselves in the only ways that they are capable of at this age (for example, by crying or screaming) or is unable to regulate themselves, we automatically say that the child is being terrible or frightening. Most parents feel that their child is rebelling for no good reason or even that the child is being completely unreasonable.

Let us take a look into how we can deal with meltdowns of a toddler this young and also what strategies can be applied into handling the rebellion.

Identifying the parent's and toddler's triggers

So, what is a trigger? Our inner child often remembers the wounds and trauma that we went through as a little one. Children who could not be co-regulated, or who were left to deal with these wounds on their own, end up developing different coping mechanisms like shouting, bottling up feelings, or even lying in order to get out of a tense situation.

As an adult, we often come across similar circumstances which remind our inner child of the trauma that it may have gone through when very young and we tend to forget that we are adults now and better at coping. The inner child instantly reacts with the coping mechanisms developed decades earlier.

These situations which elicit such reactions are known as triggers.

Parents' triggers:

With time, I came to realise that the periods when I would be at the end of my patience and ready to snap were during the nighttime routine with the child. Therapy taught me about what triggers are and how to sit with my feelings.

With this knowledge, I came to understand that it was by night that I was most triggered. I wanted the routine to end quickly and without hassles and for the child to fall asleep soon so that I would get a much needed break and me-time. Add to that the exhaustion of the entire day!

Expecting in advance that I would be triggered as the day reached its end and thus being observant of myself, prepping myself beforehand with solutions on how to deal with the child's resistance or even simple sentences to say by night, getting some me-time during the day, constantly reminding myself that the toddler has no impulse control and is not creating a mess intentionally are some of the things that help me sail through the night time in a slightly less triggered manner.

Another example of a personal trigger is when somebody is shouting. Earlier, I could not contain myself and would simply shout back. Now, I realise when shouting triggers me, and use different techniques to deal with such a situation.

So, you can start by identifying *when* you're triggered, *what* your triggers are and *how* to handle them. When you feel triggered, it is okay to take a pause/ break even if your child is upset (ensure you leave them in a safe space), tell your child that you need a few minutes, or even ask your partner to take over at such a moment and then simply sit with your emotions. Maybe you can just take lots of deep breaths. Once you feel regulated, you can go back to the child.

Child's triggers:

Ask yourself - when is my child most triggered? Often the answer to this is almost universal. When hungry or sleepy/ tired, the child is often most triggered (as it happens for lots of adults too!). Beyond this point, observing the child will help to understand better. Sharing their personal things is very very hard for a child and can be very triggering. Also wanting to assert their individual likes and dislikes in an adult household is something they find hard to navigate, especially if the adults of the house *do not* take the opinions of the child into consideration or do not know where to draw boundaries and how to stick by them.

After all, when a new human being comes into the world, it's the entire household that needs to become aware of the necessary modifications to welcome this child, who is helpless physically but whose brain is growing at a tremendous rate to equip itself and the body. With time, this baby starts experiencing multiple emotions all at once without understanding how to navigate them, and the adults around them are setting an example to the child whether they are aware of it or not. This child will see the adult experiencing various emotions and how they deal with them, whether they solve their problems or shove them under the carpet - they learn from what they see! It's that simple.

Often it is said that parenthood is about changing yourself inside out as much as it is about raising the child itself. And in this context, understanding our triggers will help us understand our *unmet* needs and also what we would need to work on, in order to meet these needs!

Making the environment a "yes" space

How best to avoid conflicts with a toddler whose will power is in the process of shaping up slowly? How to deal with a toddler who is conducting social experiments everyday to push the adults' buttons and see what happens...?

One of the first steps is to give a "yes" space to the child to express themselves and explore safely.

When I first heard of minimising the number of times we say "no", I thought "How hard can it be?". And then I realised that our inbuilt belief that children do not know anything about the world and will end up hurting themselves or else spoil whatever they touch is very strong and the one word that comes out of our mouth most often is NO!

Don't believe me?? Consciously count the number of negatives that we speak to them in one entire day and see.

One entire day.

And you will realise how many negatives come out of our mouths, directed towards our children.

She may be touching the vase and we would've shouted "You'll break it.". He's holding a glass of water and we would've yelled, "Don't spill the water.". It is not like the child has all that much control yet. I mean, isn't it easier to accept that spillage is a part of childhood? And we can keep a cloth separately for them to wipe away any spillages. That way, they will then learn to clean up after themselves too.

"Don't stamp the plastic"

"Don't touch the vessels"

"Don't talk so loud"

"Don't ask me why for everything"

The "Don't" and "No" are an immense part of our day... and theirs, unfortunately.

Think to yourself if it would help to relinquish control for some (or most) parts of the day and redirect the child instead of stating a hard "No".

"You could slip if you stamp the plastic, so be careful"

"If the vessels fall, just pick them up. I can help you with that"

"If you feel like shouting, let's go into the room and shout so that it won't disturb others in the house. It may also help you come out calmer..."

"I am tired and will respond to your WHY a little later..."

The above are examples of different ways to handle their tiny requests/ demands.

So what is a YES space?

A safe "yes" space can be a room or the house itself where dangerous objects are kept out of reach of the child and exploration can be done by the infant/ toddler freely (supervision is always recommended even in a safe environment). Sharp edges can be covered with foam and electrical sockets closed with proper child proofing. A caregiver needs to be present at all times as entire houses cannot be emptied out to give space to the child. Giving completely empty spaces may also be counterproductive as we want the child to learn to navigate their environment. Also, as adults we often wish our child doesn't fall or doesn't get hurt but this is an impossible expectation and there will be falls, tears, getting back up and getting on with their work.

Make boundaries and hold them firmly but gently

"A knife is dangerous and I cannot give it to you" is an example of a boundary.

The child will cry or say, "I just want to try it, pweaseeee" but this is a boundary that we cannot back down upon. We can comfort the child and hold them through their sadness at being denied the newly sharpened knife repeatedly, despite crying their heart out, despite their yelling or attempting to hit us in anger.

What else can we do in this situation?

❖ Validating their feelings of disappointment at being denied the object that they wanted to try so badly. "I can see how disappointed you are that the knife couldn't be given to you. However, it's very sharp and I need to keep you safe...."

❖ State the boundary and offer alternatives - like offering a knife specially meant for babies to cut veggies/ fruits or a butter knife which is not as sharp but can be used to cut through simple things.

❖ Offer a hug or cuddle as comfort. Often, detaching ourselves can help keep us calm but isn't ideal as we also end up detaching from the baby and not being able to comfort them. Validating their feelings and then offering comfort will help them truly understand what it is that they are going through at that moment. It helps build their Emotional Quotient in the long run and not turn into adults who are afraid of their own feelings.

❖ Talk to the knife itself and tell it how it is very sharp and may pierce the skin if not handled properly. Sometimes talking to the object in question can make your child focus on what's actually being said.

❖ Think clearly before setting the boundary. Is a NO really needed here? Can the child be allowed to try something under supervision?

- Try humming or whispering softly while holding them, without removing them from the situation, to give time to understand the boundary but also be able to calm down as acceptance comes in.
- Distraction as a solution to the crying can be used occasionally when we do not have the space/ time to sit with the child's feelings at that very moment. However, it is not recommended as a common strategy, as that will only serve to push away the situation for that single moment or suppress their feelings. Distracting the child will not allow him/ her to process the boundary and realise how they're feeling about it. Being there with them through the situation helps bring in the realisation faster that this is a set boundary and cannot be budged.

Go back and apologise/ repair

Let me share an example of how I, the parent, lost my cool one moment but was able to apologise/ repair it soon after.

It was already nearing my 20-month old's bedtime; she was winding down and nearing the brink of sleep but wasn't fully there yet. Part of her bedtime for a brief period was that she liked to drink water before nursing to sleep. At that time, she liked using a tumbler and a spoon (she has always loved spoons amongst cutlery). Also note that she was quite resistant to changing clothes (as are most toddlers around this age and up for some time to come).

On this particular night however, I didn't realise just how sleepy she was. I had just managed to convince said toddler to change into clean pyjamas for sleep-time and handed her the glass of water and a spoon on her request. I told her to be careful and not spill the water, *which I should've realised is something that a sleepy toddler would find very hard to do.* I was clearly setting the child and myself up for failure.

As the water from the spoon spilled onto her clothes, I lost my cool with the realisation that I would need to change her clothes all over again, which she would resist yet again. The cycle of exhaustion would just continue! I was clearly triggered by the whole incident at this point.

As she was taken aback by the sudden frustrated expression on my face, her lips quivered just a little bit and before I could gather myself, the waterworks had started.

Taking a couple of deep breaths to regulate myself, I gathered my wits about me and told myself that I could handle this. I looked at the glass that I had handed to her and realised that it was much too small. I looked at my sobbing toddler, only to realise how sleepy she was and how I could've avoided the spoon just this once! I embraced her instantly and soothed her. Then I apologised to her for not having given a bigger glass and also explained to her how sleepy she was. As I rocked her to and fro, she calmed down a little.

I then proceeded to ask if she would like to complete her glass of water with or without the spoon and the answer was a firm "No" to both. I kept the water aside and she picked up a shape sorting activity that she managed to complete twice, all by herself that night for the first time. I rejoiced with her before asking if I could now take her to bed. When she nodded her assent, I proceeded to put her to sleep.

What had I done here?? I had gotten triggered, lost my cool, become conscious of this and managed to regulate myself. I then went back and apologised to the child, finally helping her co-regulate. Even offering choices of more suitable cutlery or if she even wanted to just do something else is the next step to coregulation.

Sometimes we're enveloped in multiple layers of the things that are happening around us and fail to see situations from the toddler's perspective. They are tiny people, trying their best to cope with the strange big world, with the multiple confusing choices that surround them, while being constantly supervised by the adults who seem to do things much faster *and* much better.

Being adults who are much more capable physically and emotionally, we have to make space for a world of patience and seeing the point of view of the child before we take our next steps. It would always help to remember that the child is still learning and is doing their best at all times!

And for those times when we lose our cool and yell or cause hurt, coming back and apologising to a child will go a long way. The child will then see how mistakes can happen and what can be done to repair them! This is a valuable life lesson.

After all, it is human to err and divine to ask for forgiveness.

Strategies that help

❖ *Identifying emotions and naming them*

"I don't want to go to school!"

What is the first thing we do? Panic. We're scared that we're about to face a full-blown meltdown about the little one not wanting to go to school.

And what is it that we try to do instantly?

Convince the child that school is the best place to be right now?

Offer rewards for going to the nursery?

Punishment if the goal of marching off to play home isn't met?

How about trying a different tactic. Sit the child down and simply listen to their cry of frustration! Take a few calming breaths and say, "It looks like the thought of going to school upsets you. While I see that you learn a lot of things and come back happy, perhaps going itself isn't enjoyable to you right now?"

The toddler will most likely say yes and repeat that he/ she doesn't want to go to school. That is fine. Once they know they are genuinely understood, you can go about setting the boundary (perhaps just call it a routine) about how school will happen for the first few hours every morning.

When we feel understood, we are often in a much better place to accept the act of doing something that we aren't comfortable with.

Consider this: *A toddler's emotions are BIG in our eyes simply because* we *haven't normalised them for ourselves.*

A child starts crying and immediately chaos ensues! One person instantly tries to distract the child by making faces and offering to show toys; another person tells the child "Nothing happened, you're okay, you're okay", a third is scolding the child "you're a big boy now, big boys don't cry!" And a fourth is intoning "Stop crying, why should you cry?"

What is actually happening here? We want their tears to stop immediately. And why? Because *we* are getting triggered. It is often noted that those who weren't allowed to cry out or speak out their emotions as children get triggered when faced with similar situations as adults. So in all technicality, it is *us* adults who are feeling afraid of their big emotions and do not have the tools to deal with them. Hence we start finding any way from distracting to scaring the child to make them stop crying somehow! We aren't intimidated by the cause of the tears but the tears themselves!

Often I find that sitting down to the level of my child, allowing her to bawl her heart out while I ask her "Can I give you a hug? Did you get scared when you fell or did you hurt yourself somewhere?" helps her calm down that much faster.

Think of it this way. If I was overworked at my office and I just broke down and my manager came and told me, "You're a big girl, stop crying!" I would only want to punch him in the face. If he instead asked me, "Are you feeling stressed? Do you need a coffee break?", I would feel that much more understood. Perhaps, I would even take that small break and get back to my work feeling validated and seen.

Suppressing the little one's emotions for too long can only result in those emotions becoming trigger points. Simply sitting with them, helping them identify what they are feeling and being there for the child can enable them to become empathetic to themselves and others around them.

On this note, children can only emulate what they see. The more acceptance of emotions that we show, the more they're able to accept their own emotions and that of others better (and this only makes it easier to wade through the swamp called "life"). The more empathy we show, the better they're able to put themselves in other people's shoes and display empathy and understanding.

I had a small fall once and by the time my three year old daughter walked in, I was sitting down and crying out of pain. She asked me what happened and waited until I could gather myself enough to tell her. She then asked me to lie down, took some coconut oil and applied it to the site of the pain and asked me if I was feeling better. She then went on to tell me to be careful the next time around.

If this isn't an imitation of empathy learned by watching, I don't know what is!

❖ *Offering choices*

Imagine making decisions all the time for somebody - it can be very exhausting! On the other hand, imagine having all your decisions made for you by somebody else. That can feel so annoying.

Does this mean we allow children to do whatever they want? That would be a recipe for disaster! They don't know the world like we do. We can get them to participate in as many decisions as possible, so that they understand the world that they were born into better and also have some control of their own lives.

What sort of choices do you give? Clothes, plates, tumblers, places to sit, places to go, a specific toy while buying at a shop, etc. However it's important to remember that too many options in a choice can be overwhelming for a small child. Hence offer 2-3 items at a time when giving a choice.

At 3 or 4 months, we offered a choice of nappy to our infant by holding up one in each hand. When she stared at one of them intently, we would choose that and tell her, "It looks like you want the nappy with the stars to be put on you. I will now go ahead and help you wear it."

With a little time of offering choices wherever it is possible, the infant/ toddler is able to understand what it is they truly want.

How will this exercise help in the long run? By enabling the child to learn how to choose and also to follow their instincts. It also helps to avoid frustrations, as a child who has more control over their lives would not feel completely helpless or choiceless.

Let's say that we offer them two options in a choice and they choose an option that we aren't actually comfortable with. It helps to analyse why we aren't comfortable with something or even why we gave a choice that we aren't okay going ahead with. It is better to give options carefully; sometimes we may also need to go ahead even if the dress that the child chose to wear is *not* to our liking but was part of the offered choice.

Being genuine helps them understand that *their choice matters* even if it doesn't always make us comfortable. And their choices cannot always make us happy!

Allowing the child to make choices (or even mistakes) and learning from these mistakes under our guidance is better than us trying to control them now and the child going on to follow peers later on in life and making terrible choices then! When they learn from genuine choices followed by genuine consequences (with our support of course), they are able to make conscious decisions with care and understanding as they grow up.

❖ *Play in daily tasks*

Some days we're spending a lot of time instructing our kids to allow us to comb their unkempt hair, wash their hands after eating food while they're busy running away or even trying to tell them why their nails need to be trimmed! The amount of time and repetitions it takes can leave us feeling highly exhausted (what about parenting isn't exhausting??).

Next time around, try something that may take a few days to become routine but will become non-negotiable in the long run. Instead of "You need to wash your hands after eating", why don't you - the parent - finish your food, get up from the table very evidently and walk with exaggerated movements to the wash basin singing, "I cannot touch anything else with food on my hands. Oh sink, here I come... about to get my hands clean!"

Make it a constant act after every meal. Go and wash your hands as if the very wash basin is pulling you by a strong rope and make a nice act of wiping them dry. Soon, you will notice that your repeated behaviour (instead of repeated instructions) will make the act of cleaning up after having meals become a routine.

This is just one example of how you could make daily tasks playful. You will be able to find your own ways of doing this for various routines.

❖ *Exchanging roles*

From time to time, I tell my daughter that you are now the mamma and I'm now your child! She accepts the roles sometimes, giggles or watches me like I'm crazy. If she's not resisting, then I continue.

I become all daughter-like and complain about how hard some tasks are - like, how I ate my food but don't like to wash my hands because I hate getting wet, even if it is to clean myself. I whine about how annoying it is but needs to be done because I am not allowed to touch anything with food on my hands! She giggles or just goes back to her play.

But what I have done in the process is normalised her feelings of discomfort for her. I've led her to understand that washing hands may not be as easy as the adults make it look. By also mentioning that it cannot be avoided, I'm hoping to enable the toddler to feel her emotions yet do what needs to be done.

❖ *Preparing the toddler in advance*

Is there a change in routine today?

Is the school going to be off?

Is her least favourite person coming over?

Are you visiting somewhere with a lot of people?

Prepare your toddler.

Talking and lots of talking about who would be around, what all the child will get to see or how a particular situation will look, goes a long way into preparing them for what is upcoming, thus gaining their cooperation! If you think about it, even we adults feel more comfortable having some idea of what's ahead, rather than being thrown into the deep end constantly.

If you're taking your child to a mall, they are going to want to grab and pull all the exciting snacks, toys and other random things which they find interesting. It would help to prepare them in advance by talking about why you are going to the mall, and the list of things you are looking to buy. You can explain clearly that once you have bought these items, your shopping is done and you will be returning home. The shopping list can include something small for the child too. If they start melting down about wanting some other item, you can create a wish list with them for the future.

Be clear in your explanations. Try as far as possible to ensure that they are able to understand the significance and meaning of what you're telling them. And be concise. Long and complex descriptions and explanations will go over their head, and could even scare them.

Preparation is necessary even for unusual experiences which we expect the child will enjoy and find exciting. Take the example of a birthday party. If the child has little experience of birthday parties, they could easily be overwhelmed by the number of other children and adults, the activities, the general noise level, and the fact that someone else is getting a lot of presents while they are receiving none. Without preparation, the party could easily end in a full blown meltdown. Talking to them about what to expect and what they can do if they start feeling a certain way (and also watching them for signs of overwhelm) will go a long way.

❖ *Pretend play/ story-telling*

Oh, the versatility of pretend play!!

One can use it in any situation but remember not to become overbearing or overdo it as the child may start disliking pretend play altogether! Which would be truly sad.

The objective is to send subtle messages through pretend play or bring out hidden emotions or act out uncomfortable scenes (if need be) *along with* the toddler. The objective is not to use pretend play to bring about compliance!

There have been instances when one of the dolls had wanted to eat food alongside the toddler at the same dining table and even at the same plate. Telling the doll the importance of washing hands and not being allowed to touch anything with food smeared on its hands can help enable the little one to wash her own hands as well as the doll's hands (the water can get real for the doll too!)

Many a days, most of the animals in our "farm" have wanted to take bath in the same tub as my daughter. Most soft toys too! They even get the soap treatment (I know, I know!). However, it becomes a fun activity for the child as well as the toy-animals, so what's a little extra water and a little more sunshine to dry them out? Do consider the bonus that they come out squeaky clean too! In this scenario, you have managed to teach your child how to clean herself as well as her playthings. Agreed, there is water all around but no human or god learnt anything without creating a mess first.

When you're able to consider mess an integral part of childhood and learning, you have successfully normalised it for yourself and your little one. Factoring in "cleaning up the room" or "cleaning up the bed" before bedtime can become a routine too. You may not get help all the time from the toddler on this, especially when sleepy! There have been instances of extreme throwing when the cleaning begins, pausing the cleaning itself. On other nights, bidding "goodnight" to every toy and doll and placing them in their shelf so that they can enjoy a good rest can come to the rescue to gain a lot of help from our little elf!

Storytelling can help open up boxed emotions or details of the troublesome day too. Real stories about the situations that the adult faced that day and the emotions they faced, alongside how they eventually overcame their challenges can go a long way.

Let's say that the child had a toileting accident that day at school and ended up wetting their dress because of discomfort in communicating with the adults present there. A bedtime story of a little boy or girl who had an accident and was able to change into clean clothes can go a long way. In the story, the child is able to communicate the need for using the washroom the next day by using sign language if saying the words itself scares them.

Remember that there is no need to push a child, and storytelling simply helps them connect to their own instances or emotions and understand what they felt and what they can do. Every accident needn't become a story but we've found that stories of sharing, communicating with words, etc. have helped a great deal here.

Walk their walk, play their play.

Talk their talk, sway their way.

Raise your voice, But

Only to sing in a new way.

Become a child again today.

Will power development

Mrs. Sujata R Kumar is a practitioner of the Montessori methodology. She has studied this method of teaching for twenty years as well as worked with children for another fifteen odd years in a Montessori environment and has the below to say on will power in a child:

"Ever wonder what makes that little one get up every time they fall? Or babble so incessantly when they are learning to speak?

Well, it's nature's wonder. Nature provides a force in the child that drives all the baby's actions. So much so that the baby is either active or asleep.

This natural Power (all have it equally) is in service for babies in the first 6 years. It's very strong in the first three and in the next three years, it tapers off.

Why does it taper? Because nature has now provided 'will power', a conscious power at the baby's disposal.

The child of 3 has the task of building this will power. It comes from the baby-

* *Making choices. ALL kinds.*
* *Completing any activity taken up.*
* *Repeating activities.*
* *Waiting for their turn.*
* *Stopping movements consciously, etc.*

The will developed at this age (3-8 years) is the one that's going to help shape the child's personality, for life. What course to join? What kind of job? What field? What kind of life partner? Do we complete the activity we take up? Do we start activities that we think of?

And so much more (virtually everything in our life) is dependent on how strong our will is!

You, as parents, are in a position to impact the development of the child's will.

**Please note! This choice comes with freedom. This is useful only after the child is equipped to deal with the choice!* Freedom to make tea is of no use if I don't know how to make tea!*

Start with small choices, wherever possible, for your child.

- *Choice to put on their shoes - show them how to, not put it on for them.*
- *Choice of dress to wear (keep out 3 appropriate ones if you want) and so much more!!*

This is the tip of the iceberg. There is lots to learn and use as parents so that we can bring into the world - a Wholesome Independent Human Being.

And of course, you may hear from the society that "Your child is willful. Control him/her else they will get out of control!"

Do you think it's fair to not allow the will to grow and then expect the child to make choices confidently?

If your child is making intelligent choices, be proud. When the child is given a true choice, this child is ready to listen to reason too!!"

A lot of us grew up in households that believed that obedience was somewhere on the top of the list of the qualities of an ideal child. Growing up believing that disobedience was "bad" and thinking that the child would finally have some power upon becoming an adult are some feelings that are deeply rooted within many of us. Hence, when a child is trying to exert and understand their own will, we automatically see it as disobedience, in turn getting triggered and believing that this child who is naturally learning about his/ her decision-making capacity, is intentionally "disobeying" us. Society considers the adults' will to be greater than that of the child.

However, becoming a parent often means questioning ourselves and our beliefs at every stage of this immense journey.

If the child is unable to practise speaking their mind out, chances are that they won't be able to completely comprehend the skill of decision making. In order to fully understand circumstances and the consequences of making a decision, the child's brain needs to be able to exert its will power at several places and see what happens with the decision they're enforcing. This science experiment of speaking their mind is not just a simple experiment - every single time that their will is being exerted, the brain is watching the outcomes and learning from it.

So in reality, the child is learning to make conscious decisions and understand the impact of their choices.

Don't take the toddler's feelings personally

Like it's always said, "It's the child's right to ask for the moon; it is the parent's job to calmly state whether the moon can or cannot be given."

The toddler brain is learning immensely every second. They want to see, feel, touch and try everything they see! Does this mean they can have everything they ask for? Of course not.

The process of setting boundaries can lead to big feelings for the child, losing their calm and crying unceremoniously. Even hitting, pinching and shouting are common reactions.

Without much understanding and control of their impulses or emotions yet, they may yell or call names that they do not mean. The problem escalates when the caregiver takes this personally. It is vital to understand that the child who is screaming at the adult, has most likely seen other adults or children do the same in moments of least regulation. They are putting into practice what they have already seen.

What helps during these moments is to simply look at the child as someone who *needs* regulation at that moment. If we are triggered, it is best to analyse the root cause of our triggers and understand that the child did not personally mean to trigger us. Regulation of self is upon the adult, because the need of the moment is the presence of a calm adult who can engage in "Co-regulation" with the child. This means to be calm, accept the emotions of the child, *respond* instead of *react*, offer comfort if the child will accept it, and then bring them to a state of regulation as well.

The instant that the caregiver takes the words of the child to heart and reacts instead of responding to it, that becomes the opposite of co-regulation. It means that the child's big emotions have triggered the adult too and now there are two dysregulated persons in the environment, instead of a coregulated adult and child.

At calmer moments, it helps to sit this child down and talk strategies on what they can hit (like a pillow) or let them know that some of the words they just screamed are unacceptable for that particular family and what they can state instead. Alternatives hold a very important place in drawing boundaries. Most times, if the child is able to express their anger on a pillow or the bed, if they're able to go with a calm adult into another room and scream their heart out, it can help them understand their emotions and regulate that much better.

In summary:

- Identifying the parent's triggers and a toddler's triggers is the start to acceptance of emotions and regulation
- Making the environment a "yes" space as much as possible to avoid conflicts and toddler frustration goes a long way into minimising frustration for the child
- Make boundaries and hold them firmly but gently
- It is human to err and human to sometimes lose it. Go back and apologise/ repair and start over
- Strategies to deal with rebellions/ meltdowns include: identifying and naming emotions, offering choices, introducing play into daily tasks, preparing the child, exchanging roles, pretend play and storytelling
- Will power development is an important part of a child's growth. When we help the will power grow under our guidance, the child is able to differentiate good decisions from the not-so-good ones
- Don't take the toddler's feelings personally. Responding instead of reacting helps with co-regulation

Books for further study:

How to talk so little kids will listen, Joanna Faber and Julie King

Adult Mushroom Maintenance

Taking care of your physical and mental health

You matter, even if everyone else is focussed on the baby

Once you have a newborn in your home, it's natural that the focus is on them. Are they growing well? Are they getting the nutrition they need? What's that odd spot on their arm? Especially if it's your first child, a lot of worry can set in. And it's only too easy for everyone (including you) to lose sight of *You* and your needs. I think sometimes medical professionals have a different definition of what matters. For them, ensuring the mother and baby survive the birthing process is the priority. After that, you may well be left to handle whatever arises. I remember being in severe pain around my tailbone (which is apparently quite common, but one of those things nobody tells you about), but every time I brought it up to the medical staff at the hospital, I felt very dismissed while they focussed almost entirely on the newborn. I was left wondering why my health and well-being no longer seemed to matter to anyone. After some time, it is easy to internalise this. After all, the baby's needs are paramount, and they do require a lot of time and effort.

Physical and mental health are connected

Taking care of your health is just as important as looking after the baby. Both your physical and mental health are important, and they are connected too. Mood disorders like post-partum depression and anxiety make it much harder to eat well, stay well-hydrated, get movement into your day, and rest and sleep. And if you're unable to rest your body, then naturally it's more likely that your emotions and thoughts will go haywire. To return to the example of my tailbone pain, I can see so clearly now when I look back, how much that impacted my breastfeeding relationship with my daughter, and my overall mental health (therefore, my ability to bond with her) at the time. Nobody can function anywhere near their best when they are in constant pain.

Being primary carer of a newborn is more than a full-time job. There is the temptation to prove yourself by somehow doing all the things you used to manage pre-baby. Sometimes we are aware that we've lost a bit of ourselves and there is a strong urge to show everyone (including ourselves) that we are just as capable as before. But giving in to this urge ends up with us failing to look after our physical and emotional needs. We convince ourselves that we can be superhuman, and continue cooking, cleaning, doing laundry, looking after other dependents and everything else, while attending to the needs of an infant. However, where is the time and energy for us? There is nothing left by this point. Really, what are we trying to prove? And to whom?

The thing is, your most important work right now (other than looking after the baby) is attending to yourself. You've just grown a whole human inside of you and your body needs time - up to 3 years - and care to recover. After delivery, a dinner plate-sized wound is left in your uterus, where the placenta was attached to it. Imagine if you had such a large wound outside your body! When you have been told to rest after delivery, this is one reason why.

On top of this, hormones may be going wild, and the complete change of routine and lack of sleep can play havoc with your mood. Your heart and mind also need care. Lots of it. It's important to truly acknowledge this, and give yourself what you need. You are the only one who can do it, after all. This can be more difficult for some people than others, but overall it seems that every mother finds this challenging to a huge extent - it's hard to shake that feeling of guilt for focusing on oneself. Society does not hesitate to tell us we are being selfish or uncaring, and we are quick to believe it.

Taking care of yourself

❖ *Eating, drinking, resting is important for you as much as the child*

Let us assure you: it is okay, in fact it is good and healthy for you to focus on attending to your needs and your newborn's needs which only you can meet, and to delegate everything else to family members and other helpers. This is particularly needed in the early days, and it encourages everyone involved to feel like they are part of the village raising the baby. It is also easier to set up your support systems from the beginning than to try and change them later.

You need to eat regularly, stay hydrated, and you need to rest your body and mind. Some people struggle with these even pre-baby, and it is distressingly easy to lose track of these needs post-baby, even though they seem so basic that you could not possibly forget! And please don't fall into the trap of thinking that this kind of basic survival care is "me-time".

❖ *Having Me-time everyday*

Maybe you can't sleep when the baby sleeps (although people do love to advise that) - but you can lie down, or meditate for a few minutes, or have a peaceful cup of tea, or even go for a quick walk. Something that is for you alone. I used to read, or do word puzzles in the newspaper. Having me-time is essential for all new mothers, and even more so if you are the kind of person who recharges by being alone.

There isn't much time to spare, but it helps to regularly take what you can for yourself. The cumulative effect is huge. This is not the time to catch up on laundry or cooking (unless they are soothing for you, rather than mandatory chores). You are on call 24/7. Someone else can do the laundry. Being clear about what you can and cannot manage also normalises you caring for yourself in the eyes of everyone else. Again, it's so much easier to establish it early (perhaps even before the baby arrives) rather than try and make changes later, when you're crumbling under the load of responsibilities. Been there, done that!

❖ *Find your support systems*

Most of us don't have a "village" of people to help us raise our children. We have to make our own villages. Both of us authors are involved with a mothers' support group, and so many times we hear people saying the group is what has kept them going through the difficult phases of parenting. It's truly magical, especially when you think that most of the mothers in that group have never met in person!

You may have a neighbour who is willing and able to help out in some way, or a friend or relative who stays close enough that you can visit them for some down-time. Hired help can be a great option if it is possible for you, whether it be a nanny to help take care of the child, or someone to take over other household work such as cooking or cleaning. Day care can also be a very valuable help, if that is an option.

❖ *Find the self-care that works for you*

Amidst the emotional roller coaster that parenthood is, the sheer physical exhaustion, the slipping away of time, the wanting of patience and the lack thereof... and all the workload that repeatedly wanders into the next day's task list… how can one possibly find time for loving oneself?

There is that adorable toddler who needs your physical presence, the emotional regulation from you that he/ she doesn't have yet and gentleness but also firmness from your side. When there is so much that you have to give, give and keep giving, what must happen to the abundance inside your soul? It must feel like it's decreasing with every passing day.

This feeling of internal depletion will leave any parent frustrated and angry, overwhelmed and helpless! And this is not the ideal state to be in.

So, I ask you: what is that one thing that looks like self-care to you?

Gently rubbing that beautiful bottle of aromatic cream all over your skin?

Sitting on a chair simply staring at the rain outside?

Breathing in, breathing out?

Actions speak louder than words. We all have our own versions of rejuvenation!

Open that bottle of cream, I say! Invite your toddler to sit with you. He/ she will watch wide-eyed as you gather the cream on to your fingertips, sniff it audibly and describe its smell to your baby. They will watch as they try pulling you elsewhere but you stay firm that once the cream is slathered nicely over your body is when you will step away! They may even join in.

Make it a routine. Call it "Family care-time" or any quirky title that you want to! Everyday at the same time. Give the baby his/ her cream or share yours. Both of you apply it lovingly to your own bodies or to each other's. Whatever works.

Said toddler may lose interest in a few days but you keep at it, in the same way everyday. It will catch on and become a part of who you are and how you care for yourself.

Children simply follow what they see! If you drink enough water while explicitly saying, "My body was thirsty, my body needed water. It's feeling so much better now...", they will eventually know to follow suit. Or at the very least, they will learn to respect that you have needs that are a priority too.

Don't forget to thank your body often for creating and bringing out an entire human being from its system! Sometimes we're so focused on getting back in shape that we forget to allow our bodies time to heal and we don't thank them enough for everything that they have done so far. Give your body hugs and appreciation as often as you can. This will go a long way towards healing.

While the body needs care, what about the mind and soul?

Let me talk about this with a personal example: I need help dealing with the emotional turmoils of everyday life. Seeing my therapist on a regular basis is something that has worked wonders for my mental health. I prioritise these sessions. I have brought my family on board with this and have told them that these sessions are absolutely necessary for my mental fitness and are not expendable. My toddler has cried enough times about being separated from me during this hour but the caregiver that is in-charge of the toddler is also in-charge of the baby's emotions. As the baby slowly begins to accept that her mamma needs her "Session-time for recharge", she begins to understand what respecting mental health looks like.

It doesn't even have to be therapy sessions: it can simply be meditating or taking a walk to fill your soul with love for yourself. If you don't love yourself, how can you find the inspiration to love another wholly?

"Sacrifice" has been made synonymous with motherhood for far too long! It's time to break this downward trend and hold up the mother's health to be just as important as the baby's. After all, in order to care for my child physically and emotionally, I need to be *available* physically and emotionally right?

Neglecting your health makes it acceptable that you're dispensable

My little one fell ill. For several days. I carried her around everywhere, baby-wore her because she refused to get down. She took a long time to heal and as she began her journey to better health, mine collapsed!

As I sat in bed with severe back pain, I thought about the last few weeks that had gone by.

My child had been ill and she needed me. I gave my *all* in order to get her through. But what ultimately happened? I lost my own health and spirits over the following days. Being almost bedridden, I came to a simple realisation. While I hadn't been wrong in taking care of my little one, I hadn't done justice to my own self by not demanding timely help from the other family members. It is true that my little girl refused to go to anyone else in her sickness. At the same time, it is *also* true that I didn't set some boundaries to keep myself afloat at the very least. I let myself drown into severe pain and put my body through hell.

What did she learn through this all? That my health wasn't important enough? Or did she perceive that it was okay to sacrifice yourself in order to help somebody that you loved?

I don't think any of these messages that I may have unintentionally passed on to her can be called okay. Will they teach her to not respect my health the way it should be respected? Or worse still, will she learn to stop respecting her own body as she would assume it's okay to neglect it when there are big things that are ongoing?

Society may have forgotten teaching families to prioritise the mother's health, to realise that even new fathers undergo postpartum depression so often or to acknowledge that love is not synonymous with sacrifice! However, it is high time for us to go back to basics - eating, drinking and sleeping on time, caring for oneself as easily as caring for the child comes to us, taking whatever support is available to sail through, accepting messy houses in favour of rested bodies and being present for other parents without judgement.

After all, one cannot pour out of an empty cup.

In summary:

- *You* matter, even if everyone else at home or those visiting, are focused mostly on the baby. It's easy to lose oneself and feel unloved
- Physical health and mental health are connected. One cannot thrive without the other, hence it's best to focus on both in equal parts
- Taking care of yourself - the parent - is vital. Eating, drinking, resting is important for you as much as the child. Having me-time everyday helps keep your cup from becoming empty. Rejuvenating oneself is

an important aspect of self-care. Finding the support systems around that help during times of need is important: be it family, friends, relatives or even neighbours. Everybody's self care looks different. Hence it's important to find the self care that actually works for you

- Neglecting your health makes it acceptable to the family and the child (who is observing everything) that your health is not important enough and that it is dispensable. When we show up for ourselves and demand that our health also be prioritised, that we send the message that everybody's body, mind and soul are important and cannot be neglected

All the Rest

(Everything else related to growth of wholesome mushrooms)

Here is everything that we couldn't squeeze into the other chapters, but feels important!

The fourth trimester and baby wearing

For about the first three months of life outside the womb, babies need close contact. They need to be held a LOT. New parents are often taken by surprise when their newborns cry and cry when put down to sleep, and only seem happy when being carried. This is normal, despite all the suggestions to the contrary which you will see and hear endlessly from the rest of the world. This period is often called the fourth trimester.

You cannot "spoil" your baby and you will not create bad habits by holding your child when they need to be held. Remember, it is a *need*, not a want. And as they acclimatise to the big outside world, this need decreases in urgency. There will always be times your child wants to be held, even when they are much older - even we as adults sometimes just need a hug, right? But in these first three months, this need is most intense.

Now, nobody is saying that the primary carer of the baby should also be doing all this holding and carrying. In fact, this is one of those things which every adult in the home can participate in. For those who are not comfortable holding the baby in their arms, or who need their hands free, baby wearing in a sling or an ergonomic carrier is a great help. And it is something which can be extremely helpful well into the toddler and preschool years. It can be particularly helpful when you are travelling. Having your hands free while trying to manage bags, suitcases and paperwork is a real boon!

Running well beyond three years, the toddler and I resort to babywearing on some days when she wants to be carried and I want my hands free. These times of babywearing are special to us and we enjoy being "wound together" even if it is now for shorter durations.

Nursing/ breastfeeding

Major health bodies around the world recommend breastfeeding at least for the first two years of the child's life. There are many reasons for this recommendation, such as antibodies which pass through in the milk to the child, very easily-absorbed nutrition compared to other sources, and no need to worry about washing and sterilising equipment.

Of course this recommendation comes with many caveats - for example, breastfeeding must first be possible, and the nursing parent's life circumstances must allow for either direct breastfeeding or expressing breast milk which is later given to the child. Whatever you can give your child is great, and if you have to do combination feeding or exclusive formula feeding, this does not make you less of a mother, carer or nurturer!

Breastfeeding for two years can seem very daunting when you are starting out, but it is doable if you have enough support. I was lucky enough to be able to breastfeed my child until she naturally weaned at 4 years, 4 months. If anyone had even suggested that duration at the beginning of our journey, I would have laughed at them. But the thing is, once you get familiar and comfortable with it, it is much easier to keep going (again, assuming you have sufficient support to do so).

Do keep yourself informed. Many who have little or no knowledge in the area will be more than willing to give all kinds of advice, often about how you don't have enough milk, or you need to wean the child for one reason or the other. You are likely to receive advice such as "It's time to start Cerelac", "You're feeding the baby for too long and she will become dependent", or "The baby is crying because they are hungry. Your milk supply must be low". These are often not based in truth - a professional lactation consultant would be the best person to approach to discuss any issues which arise in your breastfeeding journey (or even your formula-feeding journey). They can determine how efficiently milk is being transferred from breast to baby, and if there are obstacles such as tongue and lip ties, which can seriously hinder breastfeeding and are also sometimes difficult to spot.

We know of an infant who was born with a slightly higher weight. She seemed happy and active initially. However, after a few weeks (even though the mother's breast milk supply had stabilised), her rate of weight gain slowed down more than would normally be expected, and she stopped pooping for longer periods than would normally be expected. Each of these individually may not have raised a major concern, but after hearing the story, a lactation consultant was able to put them together to determine that the child probably had some kind of tongue or lip tie, which another professional then assessed and confirmed.

Once the tie was released, the baby was able to nurse much better in time.

Infant Sleep

Follow baby's cues - you've heard the phrase "sleeping like a baby", right? You will soon discover that what this really means is nothing like what is implied in casual conversation (or mattress advertisements!). It is normal for babies to need breastfeeding, holding and continuous contact to sleep (baby wearing can help here too). Breast feeding to sleep is biologically normal. Melatonin generation in the body takes time, so it is only after some months that babies' bodies can differentiate between day and night.

It is normal for infants to wake regularly for feeding and comfort. In fact, methods to prolong sleep, like swaddling and the use of "jhoolas" are not recommended - we actually *want* babies to wake to nurse. Waking is protective against SIDS, and nursing regularly is important for their growth and hydration and for the nursing mother's breast milk supply to grow enough to suit the baby's requirements (if she is breastfeeding). So you can ignore anyone who tries to suggest that your baby "should" be sleeping for longer stretches, or who suggests various ways to make them sleep for longer.

We know that following the baby's lead in this matter is exhausting. Society is not set up in a way to best support parents of infants. How you manage this is dependent on you and your family setup. Some parents may take shifts, splitting the nights into halves with each parent being responsible for one half. Other couples may split duties, with one feeding and the other one burping and changing diapers. Others might have one parent doing all the night duty because they are able to rest during the day.

If you are breastfeeding, learning to nurse while lying down can be a real gamechanger. As the child becomes older, you may even find that you are able to almost sleep through nursing sessions this way! At the very least, it gives the body some rest even if you cannot sleep.

Potty learning

First, let's differentiate between elimination communication and potty learning, as this difference is often not clear.

Elimination communication (EC) is not about the child learning anything. It is when carers watch the child for cues that they are about to pee or poop, and follow up on those cues by holding the child over a potty seat or something similar. Following EC might make laundry easier but it doesn't necessarily mean that potty learning will be easier or faster for the child later on. So EC comes before the child is ready for potty learning, during the period when they would otherwise be using diapers. Anyone talking about potty learning at age 1, for example, is actually referring to EC. Whether to follow this method or not is entirely up to each set of carers. It is certainly not mandatory.

Potty learning comes into the picture later on, usually around age 2 years. It is the process in which the child learns to independently use the toilet, of course with some aids like a stool to reach things which might be too high. They would need to be physically, mentally and emotionally ready to let go of diapers, which is all they have known up to that point in their lives. Under normal circumstances, the child would be able to walk to the location, ideally be able to pull their pants up and down, clean up, flush and wash hands on their own or with a little help. Some preparation would be needed, for example talking about the process, letting the child see adults use the bathroom, and saying goodbye to diapers. Potty learning cannot be forced, but is best seen as cooperative work, just like teaching the child to do anything else.

My child almost always accompanied me into the bathroom (not every parent has to be comfortable with this, but I was okay). We often talked about how pee and potty is done in the bathroom/ toilet, sitting on the commode. As the understanding slowly set in, I began to realise that she was slowly getting ready to start potty learning post 21 months of age. There were days when she would run into the bathroom to just pee and other days when she would pee in her cloth diaper.

I took deep breaths and prepared myself mentally. I spoke to her about an upcoming trip and how we were going to stop using the nappies/ cloth diapers after coming back from the trip. This was an intensely emotional time for my daughter as well as for me. I had invested a lot of time, effort and money into researching and buying those cloth diapers and felt resistant to letting them go. However, the time for potty learning was right. The child seemed mentally prepared (well, almost). During the trip, we both said Good-Bye several times to the cloth diapers and disposables and spoke about how we would not be using them during the day (we went for potty learning during the daytime initially). Once our trip was completed, my toddler went naked waist-down for about a week and I would take her to the bathroom for every pee and poop (even if she had started them midway) and within the next 2 weeks, she began to use the bathroom during the day without any hassles.

The mental state of the parent and toddler are quite important in this journey of potty learning. Even under the ideal circumstances, it is a challenging and exhausting phase for everyone involved.

Support groups

Parenthood, particularly for primary carers, can be a lonely journey. Finding the right support group(s) for you will make a world of difference. For some people, this might mean a relative, friend or neighbour who respects your parenting decisions and supports you through them. There are online and offline options for more organised groups. For example, a well-known online community is Breastfeeding Support for Indian Mothers, and there is the La Leche League which holds in-person meetings. Both these are focused more on breastfeeding. There are also groups which offer all-round support, like Snugbub (https://www.snugbub.co.in/) with lactation experts, paediatric dentists and early childhood educators (which includes one of the authors). We both have been a part of this community since our children were infants.

There is nothing that makes a difference like knowing you're not alone in your journey, that it isn't just you or your child facing certain issues or worries. And being able to share triumphs with those who truly get the significance of them is equally amazing, and necessary!

Books for further study:

The Womanly Art of Breastfeeding, La Leche League International (LLLI)

Sweet Sleep, LLLI

The Gentle Sleep Book, Sarah Ockwell-Smith

Oh Crap! Potty Training, Jamie Glowacki

Ready Set Go, Sarah Ockwell-Smith

Conclusion to Mushroom Parenting 101

And here we are, at the end of this handbook. We hope it has been easy to read and understand and, most of all, helpful. It contains information we wish someone had shared with us before our own parenting journeys began, so ideally now you feel a bit more prepared to handle what lies ahead with some level of confidence - whether it is related to feeding, handling tantrums or taking care of yourself.

We have tried to simplify and present to you various aspects of parenting, so that you can choose which books to delve deeper into if needed, without having to feel burdened by the presence of so much parenting material to peruse!

Remember, you are the best assessor of your baby's experience. Your instincts are your first teacher. Trust your judgement and take on advice from the rest of the world with discretion. And trust your child - they are amazing at following their own bodies and expressing their needs. They only need someone who is ready to listen with some understanding, and to advocate for them.

Our children are forming precious childhood memories that will guide their reactions, their ability for empathy, their understanding through relationships and their acceptance of a full range of emotions. We, their caregivers, are responsible for shaping these formative years and what better way to do this than being conscious of available parenting styles and taking decisions based on the information privy to us??

We want to thank you for accompanying us all the way through this book. We wish you all the best as you enter this new phase of your life!

Lead with respect, dear parent
Your love can never lead you askance,
Shower an extra kiss
And feel your heart begin to dance;
Let those tiny souls
Thrive under your warm shelter
Let them remember
That you left this world that much better!

Printed by Libri Plureos GmbH in Hamburg,
Germany